First World War
and Army of Occupation
War Diary
France, Belgium and Germany

60 DIVISION
181 Infantry Brigade
London Regiment
2/22 Battalion
14 June 1916 - 30 November 1916

WO95/3032/5

The Naval & Military Press Ltd
www.nmarchive.com
Published in association with The National Archives

Published by

The Naval & Military Press Ltd

Unit 10 Ridgewood Industrial Park,

Uckfield, East Sussex,

TN22 5QE England

Tel: +44 (0) 1825 749494

www.naval-military-press.com

www.nmarchive.com

This diary has been reprinted in facsimile from the original. Any imperfections are inevitably reproduced and the quality may fall short of modern type and cartographic standards.

© Crown Copyright
Images reproduced by permission of The National Archives, London, England, 2015.

Contents

Document type	Place/Title	Date From	Date To
Heading	WO95/3032/5		
Heading	60th Division 181st Infy Bde 2-22nd Bn London Regt Jun-Nov 1916		
Heading	War Diary 2/22nd Battalion London Regiment From 14th June 1916 To 30th June 1916 (Volume 1)		
War Diary	Sutton Veny	14/06/1916	23/06/1916
War Diary	Warminster	24/06/1916	24/06/1916
War Diary	Le Havre	25/06/1916	26/06/1916
War Diary	St Pol	27/06/1916	27/06/1916
War Diary	Bethonsart	28/06/1916	28/06/1916
War Diary	Maroeuil	29/06/1916	30/06/1916
Miscellaneous	D.A.G 3rd Echelon	31/07/1916	31/07/1916
Heading	2/22nd London Regt War Diary for the month of July 1916 From 1st July to 31st July Volume		
War Diary	Ecurie	01/07/1916	07/07/1916
War Diary	Louez	08/07/1916	12/07/1916
War Diary	Ecurie	13/07/1916	15/07/1916
War Diary	Poste Lille	16/07/1916	19/07/1916
War Diary	Etrun	20/07/1916	28/07/1916
War Diary	Poste Lille	29/07/1916	31/07/1916
Miscellaneous	HQ. 181st Inf Bde		
Miscellaneous	Capt Garr Gorman		
Operation(al) Order(s)	Operation Orders No.1 By 2/22nd Battn. London Regiment	11/07/1916	11/07/1916
Heading	2/22nd Battalion London Regt War Diary From 1st August 1916 To 31st August 1916 Volume 3		
War Diary	Post Lille	01/08/1916	05/08/1916
War Diary	Ecurie	06/08/1916	13/08/1916
War Diary	Post Lille	13/08/1916	20/08/1916
War Diary	Etrun	21/08/1916	29/08/1916
War Diary	Post Lille	30/08/1916	31/08/1916
Heading	2/22nd London Regt War Diary for The Month of September 1916 From 1st September 1916 to 30th September 1916 Volume 4		
War Diary	Post Lille	01/09/1916	04/09/1916
War Diary	Ecurie	04/09/1916	10/09/1916
War Diary	Post Lille	10/09/1916	16/09/1916
War Diary	Etrun	16/09/1916	22/09/1916
War Diary	Post Lille	22/09/1916	28/09/1916
War Diary	Ecurie	29/09/1916	30/09/1916
Operation(al) Order(s)	2/22nd Bn London Regt Order No.1		
Miscellaneous	Report Of Reconnaissance From R II On The Nights Of Aug.31/Sept.1 & Sept.1st/2nd		
Miscellaneous	2/22nd London Regiment Order No.2		
Miscellaneous	181st Infy Bde	04/09/1916	04/09/1916
Miscellaneous	Report Of Raid Of 4th Sept 1916	04/09/1916	04/09/1916
Diagram etc	Diagram		
Operation(al) Order(s)	List Infantry Brigade Operation Order No.17	02/09/1916	02/09/1916
Miscellaneous	Raiding Party		
Diagram etc	Diagram		

Miscellaneous	App III	21/09/1916	21/09/1916
Miscellaneous	Amendment	03/09/1916	03/09/1916
Miscellaneous	Scheme For Trench Mortar Co-Operation		
Heading	2/22nd Bn London Regt War Diary For October 1916 From 1st October 1916 To 31st October 1916 Volume 1		
War Diary	Ecurie	01/10/1916	04/10/1916
War Diary	Post Lille	05/10/1916	10/10/1916
War Diary	Etrun	10/10/1916	16/10/1916
War Diary	Post Lille	17/10/1916	24/11/1916
War Diary	Etrun	25/10/1916	25/10/1916
War Diary	Izel-Les-Hameau	26/10/1916	26/10/1916
War Diary	Rebreuviette	27/10/1916	28/10/1916
War Diary	Neuvillette	29/10/1916	29/10/1916
War Diary	Candas	30/10/1916	31/10/1916
Operation(al) Order(s)	2/22nd London Regt Order No.22		
Miscellaneous	Headquarters 181st Infantry Brigade	09/10/1916	09/10/1916
Miscellaneous	List Of Casualties Sustained On The Night Of The Raid	08/10/1916	08/10/1916
Miscellaneous	A Report on The Events Leading Up to and Subsequent to the Deaths		
Miscellaneous	The Following Is A List Of The Names Of Those Who Acted As Covering Party And In Other Capacities		
Miscellaneous	C Form (Duplicate) Messages And Signals		
Miscellaneous	Supplementary To Preliminary Report Of The 2/22nd Battalion London Regiment's Raid	09/10/1916	09/10/1916
Miscellaneous	Preliminary Report Of The 2/22nd Battalion London Regiment's Raid	08/10/1916	08/10/1916
Diagram etc	Diagram		
Operation(al) Order(s)	2/22nd Battalion London Regiment Operation Order No.1	07/10/1916	07/10/1916
Miscellaneous	2/22nd Battalion London Regiment Appendix "A" Artillery		
Operation(al) Order(s)	2/22nd Battalion London Regiment Order No.23d	09/10/1916	09/10/1916
Miscellaneous	60th (London) Division Routine Orders	15/10/1916	15/10/1916
Miscellaneous	2/22nd Battalion London Regiment Order No.24	15/10/1916	15/10/1916
Miscellaneous	In Connection with the Relief Orders	16/10/1916	16/10/1916
Miscellaneous	60th (London) Division Routines Orders	21/10/1916	21/10/1916
Operation(al) Order(s)	2/22nd Battalion London Regiment Order No.25	22/10/1916	22/10/1916
Operation(al) Order(s)	2/22nd Battalion London Regiment Order No.27		
Heading	2/22nd London Regiment War Diary For The Month of November 1916 From 1st November 1916 To 30th November 1916 Volume 1		
War Diary	Candas	01/11/1916	04/11/1916
War Diary	Brucamps	04/11/1916	24/11/1916
War Diary	In The Train	25/11/1916	26/11/1916
War Diary	Musso	27/11/1916	30/11/1916

WO 95/2032/5

60TH DIVISION
181ST INFY BDE

2-22ND BN LONDON REGT
JUN - NOV. 1916

Vol 1

Secret.
Confidential

War Diary

2/22nd Battalion London Regiment

from 24th Sept June 1916 to 30th June 1916.

(Volume 1.)

"SECRET."

Army Form C. 2118

WAR DIARY
or
INTELLIGENCE SUMMARY
(Erase heading not required.)

2/23rd Batt. London Regt

Instructions regarding War Diaries and Intelligence Summaries are contained in F.S. Regs., Part II. and the Staff Manual respectively. Title Pages will be prepared in manuscript.

Place	Date	Hour	Summary of Events and Information	Remarks and references to Appendices
SUTTON VENY	14"		R.A.M.C. DRAFT and details of L.R.B. DRAFT completed joining the Bn. C.I. proceed on Overseas Leave. Orders for mobilization received.	Am
	15"		Overseas Leave of the Batt. completed.	Am
	16"		Interior economy - All ranks inspected by C.O. under Bn. arrangements & any deficiencies of equipment & kit made up.	Am
	17"		BRIGADE Duties during week ended 24.6.16.	Am
	18" 23"		Preparations to move occupied the Batt. this week.	Am

CONFIDENTIAL

Army Form C. 2118

Instructions regarding War Diaries and Intelligence Summaries are contained in F.S. Regs., Part II. and the Staff Manual respectively. Title Pages will be prepared in manuscript.

WAR DIARY
or
INTELLIGENCE SUMMARY
(Erase heading not required.)

1/22nd Batt London Regt

Place	Date	Hour	Summary of Events and Information	Remarks and references to Appendices
Warminster	24.6.16	1.30 p.m	The Batt. entrained at Warminster Station in 2 trains & proceeded by train to Southampton. Strength 29 Officers 951 others ranks. At Southampton the Batt. &c the Transport embarked on the Troopship "Caesaria" & proceeded to Le Havre. The Transport Section (Horses Wagons & men) proceeded to Le Havre on the Troopship "Huanchii".	am
Le Havre	25th		The Batt. disembarked at Le Havre at 7 A.M. & marched to No 2 Rest Camp. The day was occupied in cleaning & resting. All arms equipment & gas helmets were inspected & report as to deficiencies rendered to the Quartermaster.	am
Le Havre	26th		The Batt. (less C Coy) entrained at 10.30 A.M. & proceeded by train to St Pol, arriving there at 3.30 P.M. 27th met a hot meal was provided at Mont Poslin. C Coy entrained at 11.30 A.M. & proceeded by train to Petry (Cagny). The whole Batt. marched into billets at Wamerville & had breakfast	am
St. Pol	27th		The Batt. paraded again at 12.30 P.M. & marched to Behonsart & proceeded into billets for the night.	am
Behonsart	28th		The Batt. rested during the day & paraded at 4 P.M. to march to Moroeuil, halting in order to have a certain halt not earlier than 9.30 P.M. as the road then to be traversed was in range of Hostile artillery. The Batt. reached Moroeuil at 11.30 P.M. & proceeded into billets.	am
Moroeuil	29th		The Batt. rested. Orders were received that from this date onwards every man was always to carry the slung gas helmet day & night outside all equipment.	am
Moroeuil	30th		The Batt. marched into the trenches occupied by the 1st Argyle & Sutherland Highlanders & was attached to the 51st Highland Division for instruction. A & B Coys into the Right & 2 Subsectors, C & D Coys into the Left & 1 Subsectors. No casualties sustained.	am

J.R.Brocton
Major for Lt Col Commanding
1/22 London

1875 W: W593/826 1,000,000 4/15 J.B.C. & A. A.D.S.S./Forms/C. 2118.

Secret

D.A.G.,
   3rd Echelon.

   Herewith attached War Diary,
Volume 1, for the month of July 1916, of
the 2/22nd London Regiment.

                    [signature]
                         Lieut Colonel
         Comdg 2/22nd London Regiment

In the field
31st July 1916.

SECRET.

"THAMES & MEDWAY"
2/22ND LONDON REGT.

Vol 2

War Diary
for the month of
July 1916.

From 1st July To 31st July.

Volume X

SECRET
Army Form C. 2118

Instructions regarding War Diaries and Intelligence Summaries are contained in F.S. Regs., Part II. and the Staff Manual respectively. Title Pages will be prepared in manuscript.

WAR DIARY or INTELLIGENCE SUMMARY

(Erase heading not required.)

1/22nd Batt. Lond. Regt.

Place	Date	Hour	Summary of Events and Information	Remarks and references to Appendices
ECURIE	1st	a.m.	The enemy dropped about twenty shells in Ecurie Village resulting in one casualty, slight shrapnel wound. There was a fair amount of activity of Trench Mortars in the front line trenches occupied by A Coy. - One casualty only. Slight wound.	a.m.
"	2nd	a.m.	ECURIE VILLAGE quiet. Still Trench Mortar Activity along front line. Parties went out from A Coy. after dark & repaired wiring in front of trench. Heavy bombardment heard from direction of ARMENTIERES.	a.m.
"	3rd	a.m.	A Coy relieved in front line trenches by C Coy. D Coy relieved in SUNKEN Rd trenches by B Coy. Both reliefs were effected without any casualties.	a.m.
"	4th	a.m.	Rain during most of the day. Enemy quiet except for Trench Mortar activity in the trenches occupied by C Coy. One revetment badly damaged, but was repaired during the day & night. Wiring in front of the trenches tested during the night. One casualty slight shrapnel wound during the day.	a.m.
"	5th	a.m.	Bad weather continued, & communicating trenches became in very bad condition. Enemy active except C & D Coys with Trench Mortars & whizz bangs. No casualties was reported. One man (B Coy) accidentally shot through the arm through a comrade's falling down. LIEUT. C.F. ALDRICH was wounded in the foot by a shrapnel splinter. Plans of the enemy disposition were received, along the affection connected of 4th Guard Div. in left front of Guard Reserve Division in right front.	a.m.
"	6th	a.m.	Enemy quiet except for Trench Mortar activity along front line trenches occupied by D Coy. Rain at intervals during the day.	a.m.
"	7th	a.m.	Batt. relieved by 1/24 Bn Lon Regt. Relief effected without any casualties. One casualty - severe shrapnel wound received at night while returning ach Machine Gun limbers. A B & C Coys billetted in the SUCRERIE, LOUEZ, D Coy in the huts ANZIN.	a.m.

Army Form C. 2118

1/22nd Batt. Lon. Regt.

WAR DIARY
or
INTELLIGENCE SUMMARY
(Erase heading not required.)

SECRET

Instructions regarding War Diaries and Intelligence Summaries are contained in F.S. Regs., Part II. and the Staff Manual respectively. Title Pages will be prepared in manuscript.

Place	Date	Hour	Summary of Events and Information	Remarks and references to Appendices
LOUEZ	8th		The Battn. rested in billets in LOUEZ and ANZIN. With the exception of a few minor ailments, the health of the Battn. was good during the tour of duty in the trenches.	J.J.H.
	12th			J.J.H. Brigade Reserve.
ECURIE	13th		The Battn. took over ECURIE DEFENCES relieving 2/24th Bn L.R. & 2/20th L.R. in Bgde Reserve. The relief was effected without any casualties. Oun artillery bombarded enemy's trenches from 7.30 P.M. to 7.50 P.M. Many shells fell in Ecurie village from hostile howitzers. No casualties.	See operation Order No 1 J.J.H.
"	14th		Work done:- improving fire steps + revetting in fire bays at FERMES DES CAVES. Communicating trench from ECURIE CHURCH to front line improved + defuned. Fire trench from ABRI DE MOUTON to D2 improved. Own artillery shelled the enemy 1st + 2nd line trenches at 4.15 P.M, 5.15 P.M, 7.50 P.M, 10.20 P.M. Hostile artillery shelled ECURIE at 4.30 P.M. + MADAGASCAR DUMP at 10 P.M.	J.J.H.
"	15.		Work done:- No 11 Mac. gun emplacement rebuilt. Minor improvements to HIGH STREET and FERME DES CAVES. Very little artillery activity, but a few shells went over ECURIE.	J.J.H.
POSTE LILLE	16		Battn. took over right sector (from Avenue Victoire to Lille Road) from the 2 a th. The relief was effected without casualties + was completed by 6.30 p.m. At 11.45 p.m. enemy commenced a heavy T.M. bombardment on right sector, causing some damage	J.J.H.
		11.05/p.m.	At the left of the line but opposite where D Coy was, but only one casualty (killed). Our artillery got to work soon after midnight & by 1.45 a.m. things were again quiet. Later an officer's patrol went out from crater XXXIV + examined new crater A.16. c.6.7.; crater unoccupied + 35 × in diameter.	

SECRET

Army Form C. 2118

Instructions regarding War Diaries and Intelligence Summaries are contained in F. S. Regs., Part II. and the Staff Manual respectively. Title Pages will be prepared in manuscript.

WAR DIARY
or
INTELLIGENCE SUMMARY
(Erase heading not required.)

Place	Date	Hour	Summary of Events and Information	Remarks and references to Appendices
POSTE LILLE	July 16	10 p.m.	One of our listening patrols on the right flank (4341 Bryant & Pte Young) A Coy shot at and wounded a German in ref 29 (A.2.2.c.3.4.). He was brought in but did not recover consciousness. He was No 211 Heinrich Richter, 1st Gde Res Div, 64th Res. Inf. Regt. This was S. of line recently held by this Regt, & should have been in area of 1st Gde Res Regt. With reference to this event the G.O.C. sent the following special notice to the Bn :— "The G.O.C. congratulates the 2/22 London Regiment on being the first to kill and gather a German. He considers this a very creditable performance. The information gained was of the greatest importance & was what G.H.Q. have been trying to find out." The Brigade sent :— "With reference to the above the Bde thoroughly endorses the G.O.C.'s remarks." ~~An officer reader & men enter patrol~~ fortes began to the Bonnet Trench widened and ~~repaired~~	See Appendix A. J.7.H J.7.H
	17		An officer's patrol went out to examine a crater 50 x N. of ref 28, & heard enemy putting up wire beyond crater. Party returned at 1 a.m. There was considerable hostile trench mortar activity during the morning. Hostile artillery damaged the S. end of Fontaine & Morton Avenue between 4 – 6 p.m., & also Collecteur. Enemy scored a direct hit on Stokes gun at 3 p.m. in Ott avenue ~~trench~~ erected in Collecteur Trench 2.14–7.12. J.7.H	J.7.H

Army Form C. 2118

WAR DIARY
or
INTELLIGENCE SUMMARY
(Erase heading not required.)

Instructions regarding War Diaries and Intelligence Summaries are contained in F. S. Regs., Part II. and the Staff Manual respectively. Title Pages will be prepared in manuscript.

Place	Date	Hour	Summary of Events and Information	Remarks and references to Appendices
POSTE LILLE	July 19		Usual T.M. activity of enemy in morning.	J.7.H.
Étrun	20		Blue German uniform & hat seen from crater xxxiv	
			Minor repairs to BONNAL TRENCH & work on 2 snipers' loopholes.	J.7.H.
		J.7.H	Usual T.M. activity, promoted by ours. Usual T.M. activity. 10 retaliations.	
			Bn rested. came into billets on left. arrival of draft of 50 from 10th London Regt. morning, rgt. on left.	apt. B
	21		Bn rested.	J.7.H
	22		Bn rested. Concert at 8 p.m. J.7.H	J.7.H.
	23		Sunday. Church Parade 10 a.m. J.7.H	J.7.H.
	24		Bath. Did short route marches by platoons & physical drill. Snipers fired on range.	J.7.H.
	25		Same as day before J.7.H	J.7.H.
	26		" " Concert 7.30 p.m. Order that tin helmets to be worn on all occasions.	J.7.H.
	27		Machine gun section went up to the trenches	J.7.H.
	28		Bn took over subsector night 2 from the 2/24 Lond. R. The relief was completed about 4.30 p.m. w. on Shooters & Wick Avenues, M.30 & the junction of Bonnal & New without casualties by 5 a.m. A Coy went on right, C on centre, Bon left, & D Coy in support. Night was quiet	J.7.H.
POSTE LILLE	29		Our artillery bombarded enemy lines from 5 p.m. to 5.20 p.m. Hostile artillery and Trench mortars were active at intervals throughout the day, especially Fontaine. Two patrols went out one from crater xxxiv, the other from cpt 29.	J.7.H.

Army Form C. 2118

WAR DIARY
or
INTELLIGENCE SUMMARY
(Erase heading not required.)

Instructions regarding War Diaries and Intelligence Summaries are contained in F. S. Regs., Part II. and the Staff Manual respectively. Title Pages will be prepared in manuscript.

Place	Date	Hour	Summary of Events and Information	Remarks and references to Appendices
POST LILLE	29 July		Work was continued on Bernal & Callaghan trenches. Our casualties were 3 killed and 2 wounded. The night was quiet. Enemy ballonnet during day.	J.7.H.
"	30 July		One of our patrols shot a German on Exeter 70 x N.E of crater XIV. Very little activity.	J 7 H
"	31 July		T.M. & artillery activity on both sides about 5 a.m. Day otherwise quiet.	J 7 H

Caluck Dul

Appendix A.

HQ 181st Inf Bde

The GOC congratulates the 2/2 London Regt on being the first Battalion to kill & gather a German. He would like to know the names of the men who were instrumental in this creditable performance. The information gained was of the greatest importance & was what General Headquarters have been trying to find out.

HQ 60th Divn
17.7.16

(Signed) C.T. Humphreys
Lieut Col
General Staff.

OC 2/2 London Regt.

With reference to the above, the Brigadier in charge endorses the GOC's remarks. (Please forward names officially.)

(Signed) J. Horlick
Capt.
Brigade Major
181st Inf Bde

Capt Carr Gowen
Capt Dodge
Lieut Huntington

OPERATION ORDERS NO. 1.
by 2/22nd Battn. London Regiment.

Appendix B

1. The 181st Infantry Brigade will relieve the 154th Infantry Brigade on the 13th July 1916.

2. The 2/22nd Battalion London Regiment will ~~relive~~ relieve ½ the 2/23rd Battalion and ½ the 2/24th Battalion at ECURIE and Brigade Reserve on Thursday 13th inst.

3. The 2/22nd Battalion moving up by platoons at 5 minutes intervals will pass ANZIN CHURCH as follows, and proceed via Up Trenches.

    "D" Company and 1 Lewis Gun for SUNKEN ROAD, the leading platoon passing at 1 p.m.

    "A" Company and 1 Lewis Gun for ABRI CENTRAL, leading platoon passing at 1-20 p.m.

    "C" Company ~~and 1 Lewis Gun~~ for ABRI MOUTON, leading platoon passing at 1-40 p.m.

    "B" Company and 6 Lewis Guns for ECURIE, leading platoon passing at 2 o'clock.

    Headquarters for ECURIE Headquarters, passing at 2-20 p.m.

4. Guides of the 4th Gordon Highlanders will be met at ANZIN CHURCH to guide platoons to their positions.

5. The following details will proceed to the trenches 24 hours before the relief. Lewis Gun Officer, 1 Sergt. and 2 men per Company to be detailed by 2/Lt.C.C.ROSE. The Signalling Officer and 2 men per Company to be detailed by Capt.L.B.HODGE.
2/Lt.ROSE will report to Major HUNT at Headquarters ECURIE at 11-30 a.m. on the 12th inst.
These parties will be rationed until the morning of the 14th inst.

6. The unexpended portion of the day's rations will be carried, and the Transport Officer will arrange for the rations for the 14th inst. to be brought up to the advance dumps at on the night of the 13th - 14th July.

(Signed) ALFRED MAYER

Captain & Adjutant.
2/22nd Battalion London Regiment.

11th July 1916.

Secret.

2/2nd Battalion London Regt.

War Diary.

From 1st August 1916
To 31st August 1916.

Volume X

WAR DIARY
or
INTELLIGENCE SUMMARY

(Erase heading not required.)

Army Form C. 2118

Instructions regarding War Diaries and Intelligence Summaries are contained in F.S. Regs., Part II. and the Staff Manual respectively. Title Pages will be prepared in manuscript.

Place	Date	Hour	Summary of Events and Information	Remarks and references to Appendices
POST LILLE	1/8/16		Usual artillery and trench mortar activity.	J.7.H.
"	2/8/16		Successful retaliation of our field guns & T.M. several times to hostile fire.	J.7.H.
"	3/8/16		Day quiet. Wick Avenue, 500 Avenue, and Bomal M.3.3-34 completely damaged by enemy T.M. 1.30-2.0 p.m. & again at 7.30 p.m.	J.7.H.
"	4/8/16		A relief took place opposite our right between 10 p.m. & 1 a.m. Night unusually quiet.	J.7.H.
"	5/8/16		Batt. relieved by 2/24 Lond. R. & went into support at Ecurie. Relief completed without accident by 3 p.m.	J.7.H.
ECURIE	6/8/16		Batt. in Bde Reserve at Ecurie.	J.7.H.
"	7/8/16		2nd Lts Murrane & Fotheringham joined the Bn. from the 3rd line.	
	8/8/16			
	9/8/16			
	10/8/16			
	11/8/16			
	12/8/16			
POST LILLE	13/8/16		Batt. relieved 2/24 Lond. R. in night II. Relief completed without accident by 6 p.m.	J.7.H.
"	14/8/16		Usual T.M. & artillery activity. Successful retaliation several times by our Stokes guns & T.M.'s.	J.7.H.
"	15/8/16		No incident to report.	J.7.H.
"	16/8/16		Enemy working party disturbed opposite crater XXXIV. Our artillery & T.M.'s bombarded enemy trench system in A.2.3.a at 9.30 p.m.	J.7.H.
"	17/8/16		Enemy working party again disturbed opposite crater XXXIV.	J.7.H.
"	18/8/16		No incident to report. Corps artillery active all night in front of brigade to our left.	J.7.H.
"	19/8/16		Our artillery active on the right.	J.7.H.
"	20/8/16		Our artillery active & gas employed in front of division on our left.	J.7.H.

WAR DIARY or INTELLIGENCE SUMMARY

Army Form C. 2118

Place	Date	Hour	Summary of Events and Information	Remarks and references to Appendices
ETRUN	21/8/16		Bn. came out into rest billets & was relieved by 2/24 Lond. R. Relief completed without casualty by ~~about~~ 8 p.m. 2nd Lt. C. C. Rose left for England to join the Machine Gun school at Grantham. 2nd Lt. Thow & a draft of 100 men from the L.R.B. joined the battalion.	J.F.H.
"	26/8/16		Bn. rested in billets	J.F.H.
"	26/8/16		Capt. Eastwood joined the Bn. from the 3rd line.	J.F.H.
"	27/8/16		2nd Lt. E. Rose joined the Bn. from the 3rd line	J.F.H.
"	29/8/16		The Bn. relieved the 2/24 Lond. R. in right II. Relief accomplished without casualty.	J.F.H.
POST LILLE	30/8/16		Bad weather interfered with operation.	J.F.H.
"	31/8/16		Large working parties in repairing & cleaning of trenches. Artillery & T.M.'s cut wire in places. 2nd Lts. Arnold, Dowdall, Le Chavetois, & Schofield joined the Bn. from the 3rd line.	J.F.H.

Calvert Lt. Col.
Commanding 2/22 Lond. R.

SECRET.

Vol 4

2/22nd London Regt

War Diary
for the month of
September 1916.

From ..... 1st September 1916
To .... 30th September 1916

Volume 1.

WAR DIARY
or
INTELLIGENCE SUMMARY
(Erase heading not required.)

Army Form C. 2118

Place	Date	Hour	Summary of Events and Information	Remarks and references to Appendices
POST LILLE	1/9/16		A patrol of ours twice penetrated the German lines near LILLE ROAD. For results, see appendix I. were communicated to the roops, see appendix I.	Appx. I J.7.H.
"	2/9/16		Our T.M's effectively cut enemy wire at A.2.9.6.60.25	J.7.H.
"	3/9/16		No incident to report.	J.7.H.
"	4/9/16		At 3 a.m. a raiding party of 2 officers (2nd Lt Stephens & 2nd Lt Smith), 3 N.C.O.'s & 24 men raided the enemy lines at A.2.2.a.9.9. The enemy's wire had not been sufficiently cut for the party to enter. For the orders issued see appx. II. Our party had one casualty.	Appx. II
			The 2/22 Lond. R. was relieved in Right II by 2/24 Lond. R. & went into Bde. reserve at ÉCURIE; relief accomplished without casualty by 4 p.m. 2nd Lt. Seddon joined the Bn. from the 3rd line.	
ÉCURIE	4/9/16 to 10/9/16		Batt. J.7.H. was in Bde. Reserve at ÉCURIE.	J.7.H.
POST LILLE	10/9/16		Batt. relieved 2/24 Lond. R. in Right II. Relief completed without casualty in spite of some shelling.	J.7.H.
"	11/9/16		Our mortars bombarded enemy lines to N. of LILLE ROAD at 11 a.m. 5 casualties O.R.	J.7.H.
			2nd Lts Kinnow and T. Law killed in action. Casualties O.R. 1.	
"	12/9/16		Our artillery & T.M's active on enemy's wire at intervals along the whole front.	Appx III J.7.H
"	13/9/16		Wire cutting continued to S. of salient. Our Stokes gun active on crater XIX during the night	J.7.H.
"	14/9/16		No incident to report.	J.7.H.
"	15/9/16		The 2/22 Lond. R. was relieved in night II by 2/24 Lond. R. & went into next billets at Etrun. Relief completed without casualty.	J.7.H.
"	16/9/16			J.7.H.

Army Form C. 2118

WAR DIARY
or
INTELLIGENCE SUMMARY
(Erase heading not required.)

Place	Date	Hour	Summary of Events and Information	Remarks and references to Appendices
ÉTRUN	16/9/16 to 22/9/16		Battalion rested Sept 20th 2nd Lt. P. C. Taylor joined the Battn. from the 3rd line.	
POST LILLE	22/9/16		Bn. relieved 2/24 Lond. R. in Right ½ II. Casualty O.R.I (accidentally killed).	
"	23/9/16		Our 2" mortars cut wire between A.22.a.8.9 and A.22.b.1.8. Recent bad weather caused much work on the Bernal to be necessary throughout during the whole of this tour of duty in the trenches.	
"	24/9/16		Our heavy artillery and T.M.'s bombarded the enemy trenches between Argyle Crater and crater XXXIV. It was learnt today that the 72nd regt. 8th div. of IX Corps, who had been opposite us, had been recently relieved by the 71st divisioner IX corps; regiment as yet unknown.	
"	25/9/16		Six patrols went out during the night & made reports on the enemy wire.	
"	26/9/16		No incident to report.	
"	27/9/16		Marked M.G. activity on both sides during the night.	
"	28/9/16		Battn. went into Bde Reserve at ÉCURIE & was relieved in night II by 2/22 Lond.R. Relief completed without casualty.	
ÉCURIE	29/9/16		2nd Lt. L. G. B. Hill joined the bn. from the 3rd line.	
"	30/9/16		No incident to report.	

2/22nd Bn London Regt.
Order No. 1.

Ref: Roclincourt 51B. N.W.1. Edition 2c Scale 1:10000 + Trench Maps.

1) A raid will be made by a party from B coy at a time to be known as zero on the 4th September 1916.
2) Object: To obtain identifications and information of the enemy's trenches
3) Objective A 22. a 93. 92.
4) Jumping off point Sap 30 A.
5) The party will consist of 3 groups A. B & C under the command of Sec. Lieut Stephens.
   A + B groups. The duty of these groups after reaching points of ingress to form bombing blocks on both flanks and to cover the advance and retirement of C group.
   C group under Sec Lieut Smith to advance up trench selected for the raid.
6) Sec Lieut Stephens will issue his own orders for the disposition of groups A.B & C (Copy attached).
7) Fourth group under Lieut Hayford will hold Sap Head 30a and Crater XXV and throw out connecting files to point of ingress
8) At the time to be known as Zero the party will leave Sap Head 30a in the order A. B and C.
9) The Signal of withdrawal at +20 will be a shower of red rockets from the Centre Coy, Advanced + main H.Q.
10) The Signal that the raiding party has arrived back in our lines and which will also be the signal for cease fire will be a shower of Green, white, green, white, green, white, rockets.
11) The wire will be finally cut by the T.M. Batteries on the afternoon of the 3rd September. At + 5 mins the artillery will bombard the enemy T.M. positions + support line until the cease fire signal is sent up.
12) Feint bombardments will be carried out by the T. M's
13) An advanced telephone station will be established in the vicinity of SAP 30A.
14) Advanced Medical Aid posts will be established at the junction of the Bonnal + Sap 30.
    Casualties will be evacuated direct via Sutherland Avenue to Ariane.
15) Pass word will be "Bermondsey" answer "Thames".
16) The watches of all concerned will be synchronised at 5 pm on the 3rd September.
17) There will be no movement in the Bonnal from -30 minutes until cease fire and down traffic will make way for all up traffic, in communication trenches.
18) The party will be allotted special dug-outs in the Bonnal to which they will return on completion of the raid.
19) Zero time will be notified later.
20) ACKNOWLEDGE

C.A Lush Lieut Colonel
Comdg 2/22nd London Regt.

REPORT OF RECONNAISSANCE FROM R II
on the Nights of Aug.31/Sept.1 & Sept. 1st/2nd.

Names of men forming patrol -

    Pte. THOMAS,   A Coy.   2/22 Lond.R.
    "   SMITH,   C "   2/22 " "

I.   Patrol started at 8.30 p.m. from Crater XIV.
       Objective - To reconnoitre enemy's wire on either side
             of LILLE ROAD.

       Crossing to the E. of LILLE ROAD, the patrol continued some 60^X up an old ditch running parallel with the road some 15 - 20^X E. of it, until voices were heard distinctly of men coming down a sap to the W. of the road in the direction of our lines. The patrol was uncertain whether they were friends or enemies and moved forward inclining rather to the N. to a point nearer them. The party proved to be a team of German machine gunners firing from a bay in an enemy sap apparently running straight out from their lines. The patrol then took a wrong and easterly direction, and reached what the second reconnaissance (q.v.) showed to be a German trench. They eventually got back to the BONNAL just to W. of the LILLE ROAD. While returning, they heard the above-mentioned Machine Gun open fire and formed the opinion that it could sweep round from N.W. to S.W. The condition of the ground to within 20 or 30^X of the road on either side is very uneven, full of shell holes and craters. For condition of wire, see II.

II.   The second reconnaissance was undertaken at 5.30 a.m. Sept. 1st by the same patrol with the object of confirming the information obtained overnight.
       Starting from a point in BONNAL to E. of LILLE ROAD, they crossed some old trenches and worked towards position of Machine Gun. On reaching the nearest point on the E. of the road to the emplacement, they crossed to the W. of the road and saw the emplacement clearly with the sap running from it to the German lines. Then recrossing to the E. of the road they followed an old trench parallel with it for some 40 or 50^X, and then took a more N.E. direction. Eventually they came to a trench quite 8' deep, which they supposed to be the support trench, i.e. the second from the front. THOMAS was able to get in at a point where a shell hole caused a slide. Each side of the trench was lined with a lath frame worked close; comparatively new trench boards were along the bottom; the trench was untraversed and had no sandbagged parapets or parados, which were partly concealed by grass.
       Re. wire, they report 3 lines. (1) 30 to 40^X in front of front line - low and strong. (2) Just in front of front line in masses of tangled wire. (3) Just across the trench, even stronger wire. Just across the LILLE ROAD and some 30^X E. of it they report the wire very weak.
       Fires were observed along the German second line.

III.   At 5 a.m. Sept. 2nd, same patrol went out to Crater XIX^a (A.22.b.2.5) and found wire very thick. A heavy report was heard in the direction XIX, decidedly behind it. They opined this was a T.M. with approximate co-ordinate A.22.b.2.6.

                                 (signed) J.F.HUNTINGTON.
                                           Lieut.
                              Intelligence Officer, 2/22 Lond.R.

SECRET Appendix II
2/22nd London Regiment
ORDER NO 2

1) A RAID will be carried out by a party from "B" coy on the night of the 9/10 SEPTEMBER at a time known as ZERO.

2) ZERO = 3 am.

3) At + 20, a shower of RED very lights will be fired to recall the RAIDING PARTY, upon the return of the party the CEASE FIRE signal will be notified by the firing of SIX rockets in the following order GREEN, WHITE, GREEN, WHITE, GREEN WHITE, when the ARTILLERY will CEASE FIRE (these signals will be fired by the Batt. Bombing Officer). CAPT LIDDIATT the Bde Bombing Officer will arrange to fire WHITE VERY LIGHTS at one minute intervals from the SAUSAGE REDOUBT, ECURIE, commencing one minute after the recall signal, and continuing until the CEASE FIRE signal.

4) At ZERO all ranks who are not engaged in special work will be, as far as possible under cover, and standing by for emergencies, with a sentry on each DUGOUT, each S.O.S. rocket stand, will have a special man told off whose duty it will be to fire the rockets in case of necessity.

5) The return to NORMAL CONDITIONS will be notified to O.C coys by "BULLY BEEF NOT AVAILABLE".

6) If prisoners are taken Battn Headquarters will immediately be notified as to numbers and regiment, and arrangements will be made between Battn Intelligence Officer and OC "B" coy for them to be immediately taken to the "ADVANCED DRESSING STATION" in the GENEE DOWN TRENCH.

7 All TELEPHONE WIRES will be kept clear from 2.45 am until NORMAL CONDITIONS, except for urgent PRIORITY messages.

8 O.C coys will detail 2 Stretcher Bearers & 1 Stretcher to stand by in readiness to proceed immediately to M30 in the BONNAL if required

9 ACKNOWLEDGE.

       Signed A Mayer Capt + Adjt
        2/22nd London Regt.

1–4 Copies sent O's C coys
  5   Files
  6   War Diary.

H.Q.
   181st Infy Bde.

A copy of the report by 2nd Lt
F.J. STEPHENS in command of the
raiding party this morning is attached.

Want of time alone, both in
preparation and carrying out the raid
was the cause of the failure of the raid.

The morale and discipline of the
party was excellent and no blame attaches
to the Officers, 2nd Lt F.J. STEPHENS and 2nd
Lt E SMITH that the raid failed

All details connected with the raid
worked smoothly especially the signalling

4-9-1916

Lieut Colonel
Comdg 2/22nd London Regt

Report of Raid of 4th Septr 1916
by
2/Lt F.J. Stephens + 2/Lt E. Smith

On the 4th Septbr 1916 at 3 am a raiding party consisting of 29 NCOs and men under the command of myself and 2/Lt Smith, left SAP 30A and proceeded towards the Enemy lines in the direction of B.

About 1 minute after starting we were fired on by a sniper directly to our front. No 2476 Pte A S HATHERWAY was wounded in the right foot.

I immediately detached 3 bombers to deal with the sniper, and leaving disused trench went forward with the remainder of the party.

On approaching the enemy lines we were bombed from the right and left – presumably from their front trench.

Proceeding on our way, we entered another disused trench at C, and approached to within 5 yards of the enemy parapet where we found the wire too thick to penetrate.

While searching for a suitable point to get through two or three enemy bombs exploded on our right.

We retaliated – then, finding an

opening in the wire on the left, I was leading my party through the SAP, when the signal to retire was observed.

I therefore withdrew my party, after throwing several bombs which exploded at different points in the Enemy front line.

The whole party returned safely.

In my opinion the enemy trenches were very lightly held at this point - possibly by one or two bombers or snipers

(Sd) F.J. Stephens 2nd Lt

L/Cpl T.L. Barden, one of 3 bombers left behind to silence the sniper, reports disused trench barricaded with sandbags at point D in his opinion this barricade having been constructed since our reconnaissance on the previous night.

L/Cpl Barden threw a bomb at supposed position of sniper, who did not fire again

(Sd) F.J. Stephens 2nd Lt

The Very Lights fired from the "SAUSAGE" redoubt were observed, and had the guiding tape broken would have proved of much use in guiding the party back.

(Sd) F.J. Stephens 2nd Lt

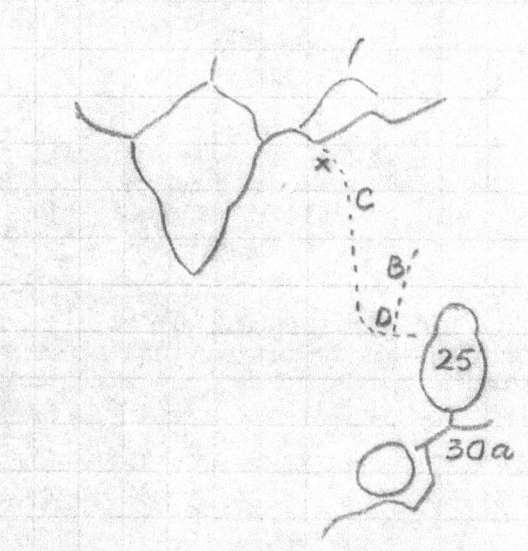

x = Point reached by leading men of raiding party.

SECRET Copy No... 6

ON NO ACCOUNT IS ANY TELEPHONE MESSAGE TO BE SENT WITH
REFERENCE TO THESE ORDERS PRIOR TO ZERO.

181ST INFANTRY BRIGADE

Operation Order No.17
------ooo---ooo------

Reference:-
51B N.W.1 Edition   Headquarters,
2C 1/10,000   181st INFANTRY BRIGADE
TRENCH MAPS   2nd September 1916

1. The 2/22nd Bn. London Regt. will carry out a Raid on the enemy's trenches at A.22.a.93.92 in the early morning of 4th September 1916, with the object of securing a prisoner and causing damage to the enemy.

2. The Raiding Party will consist of
   2 Officers
   3 N.C.O's   24 Privates

3. The O.C. 2/22nd Lond. R. will arrange all details as to the Infantry Operations in so far as they concern the Raiding Party and all other troops in his sub-sector, who will be entirely under his tactical command during the operations.

4. THE O.C.181st MACHINE GUN COMPANY will arrange to sweep with fire the main German communication trenches, tramways, and any portions of the German second line that he can enfilade. He will fire his usual call/until "Cease Fire" signal.

5. The O.C. RIGHT GROUP ARTILLERY will issue all orders as to Artillery co-operation, saps to be cleared as O.C.2/22nd Lond. R. may direct.

6. For TRENCH MORTAR CO-OPERATION SCHEME see Appendix "A" attached. O.C. Subsectors to arrange with O.C.Trench Mortars as to which Saps it may be necessary to clear. All Saps will be cleared by - 15 minutes. O.C. 2/21st and 2/22nd Lond. R. to arrange for dug outs for Trench Mortar teams to stand by in.

7. The Operations will commence at a time to be notified later called "ZERO"; at ≠ 20 minutes a shower of RED rockets will be fired to recall the Raiding Party. Upon the return of the party the "Cease Fire" signal will be notified by the firing of 6 rockets in the following order :- GREEN WHITE GREEN WHITE GREEN WHITE when the Artillery will cease fire.
Captain LIDDIATT the Brigade Bombing Officer will arrange to fire WHITE Very lights at 1 minute intervals from a point to be selected by him in the SAUSAGE REDOUBT, ECURIE commencing 1 minute after the "Recall" signal and continuing until the "Cease Fire" signal, he will then stand by. T.F.O.

8. At ZERO all men of "A"(2/21) "B"(2/22) and "C"(2/24) Battalions who are not engaged in special work will be as far as possible under cover, and standing by ready for emergencies, with a sentry on each dug-out. Each S.O.S. rocket stand will have a special man told off, whose duty it will be to fire the rockets in case of necessity. O.C's R.I(2/21) and R.II(2/22) will use their own discretion as to when they consider it advisable to return to normal conditions, and will inform Brigade Headquarters on so doing, by sending the code message "Your BM.100 acknowledged" The O.C. ECURIE GARRISON (O.C.2/24) will be informed of the cessation of "Stand to" by Brigade Headquarters by the same signal.
                                                        contd

-2-

9. The O.C. 2/21st Lond. R. holding R.I will arrange to assist the Raid with Lewis Guns fire and rifle grenades.

10. The O.C. 3/3rd Field Company R.E. will arrange that all men under his command are clear of the trenches by 1 a.m. 3/4th September 1916. He will warn the O.C's of any Army or Corps R.E. who may be working in the Sector to this effect.

11. If prisoners are taken Battle Brigade Headquarters will be immediately informed as to numbers and regiment, they will be taken to Advanced Dressing Station ANZIN G.7.b.8.9. under Battalion arrangements via GENIE d down trench, where they will be handed over to an officer of the 2/23rd Lond R.(to be detailed by the O.C. 2/23), who will immediately bring them to Rear Brigade Headquarters in a car that will be provided for the purpose, and report to the Staff Captain who will immediately inform Divisional Headquarters by telephone. The Officer detailed for this duty will report to the Staff Captain for instructions at 6 p.m. on the 3rd inst.

12. O.C. 2/22 Lond. R. will make all necessary arrangements for the synchronization of watches.

13. Every effort will be made to ensure constant reports as to progress being forwarded to Brigade H.Q., a detailed report as to the operations to reach Brigade H.Q. by 1 p.m. 4th September 1916.

14. All reports will be sent to REAR BRIGADE H.Q. ETRUN during the operations. Written dispatches via Battle Brigade H.Q.

15. Acknowledge.

16. The O.C.185th Tunnelling Coy. R.E. will arrange that all men of his Coy. are in their dug-outs by 1am. The portion of his Coy at CHEMIN CREUX coming under the orders of O.C.2/21st Lond R. for tactical purposes. The portion at BLANC coming directly under the orders of G.O.C. 181st Infy. Bde. If conditions are normal work may be recommenced at 6 a.m. The O.C.185th Tunnel Coy. will be informed by Brigade Hdqtrs. when conditions are normal.

            Captain
           Brigade Major
          181st Infantry Brigade

Issued by Orderly
	Copy No.		
C	1	Division "G"	
	2	C.R.A.	
	3	A.D.M.S.	
	4	179th Infy. Bde.	
	5)		
	6)	2/22 Lond. R.	From 15 to close of
	7)		operations all lines
	8	2/21st Lond. R.	will be kept clear,
	9	2/23rd Lond. R.	except for messages of
	10	2/24th Lond. R.	a tactical nature.
	11	181 M.G.Coy.	
	12	181 T.M.Battery	
	13	Z.60 T.M.Battery	
	14	Rt. Group Artillery	
	15	3/3rd R.E.	
	16	185th Tunnel. Coy	
	17	38th C.I.H.	
	18	Staff Captain	
	19	Filed	
	20	War Diary.	

to be let know zero

1. **Raiding Party** under 2/Lt Stephens in command, and 2/Lt Smith second in command:—
   Party divided into 3 Groups A 1 NCO and 7 men B 1 NCO and 7 men
   Commanded by 2/Lt Stephens
   C 1 NCO and 8 men commanded by 2/Lt Smith
   2 Ladder men.

2. Groups A and B will each consist of:—
   2 Front Bayonet men 1 Carrier (with wire mattress) 2 Bombers
   1 NCO in charge 2 Rear Bayonet men.
   2nd Lt Stephens in Command of above.
   Group C will consist of:—
   2 Front Bayonet men 2 Bombers 1 NCO 2 Carriers 2 Rear Bayonet men
   2nd Lt Smith in command.

3. Party will proceed in the following order A Group B Group C Group
   2 Ladder men.
   Arms Each Bayonet man will carry rifle with fixed bayonet – 9 rounds in magazine, 1 in chamber, and 2 spare clips in right hand pocket – also 2 bombs in left hand pocket.
   Bombers and carriers will each carry 10 bombs.
   NCOs will be armed similarly to Bayonet men.
   Ladder men will each carry 2 bombs.
   In addition every man will carry a Knob Kerry.

4. All men will wear steel helmets, no equipment will be worn, and no gas helmets carried.
   Faces darkened. White on shoulder strap
   Special identity discs will be issued. All means of identification such as badges – Private letters – marks on clothing etc, will be removed.
   <u>Stores required</u> 110 bombs, 29 Knob Kerries, 2 Wire mattresses, 6 wire cutters, 30 yards strong cord, 2 ladders (8 ft long) 6 pair wiring gloves.

5. At time known as Zero party will leave Sap head 30A in the order A.B.C followed by 2 Ladder men, and skirting left of Crater 25, proceed along disused trench to point M. Group A leaving disused trench will enter enemy trench at point N, where they will block trench. At the same time Group B will turn half left and proceed until they reach communication trench at O. They will continue along parapet entering trench at P, then working backwards block trench at Q. If possible 2 bayonet men and 1 bomber will then work along trench to T, returning to Q. Simultaneously Group C will enter at O and proceed up communication trench R.

   ☆ At the signal to retire, Group C will be the first to withdraw, followed by B, followed by A.
   The Officers will count their men as they leave enemy trench.

6. The signal to retire will be a shower of red rockets. Directly this is observed, the code word CRATER should be passed along to each man of party.
   Password will be BERMONDSEY answered by THAMES.

   ☆ Note After raiding party have entered enemy trench – the two ladder men will remain on parapet to guard ladders, and to improve ways of withdrawal.

(Sd) J J Stephens 2/Lt
2/22nd London Regt.

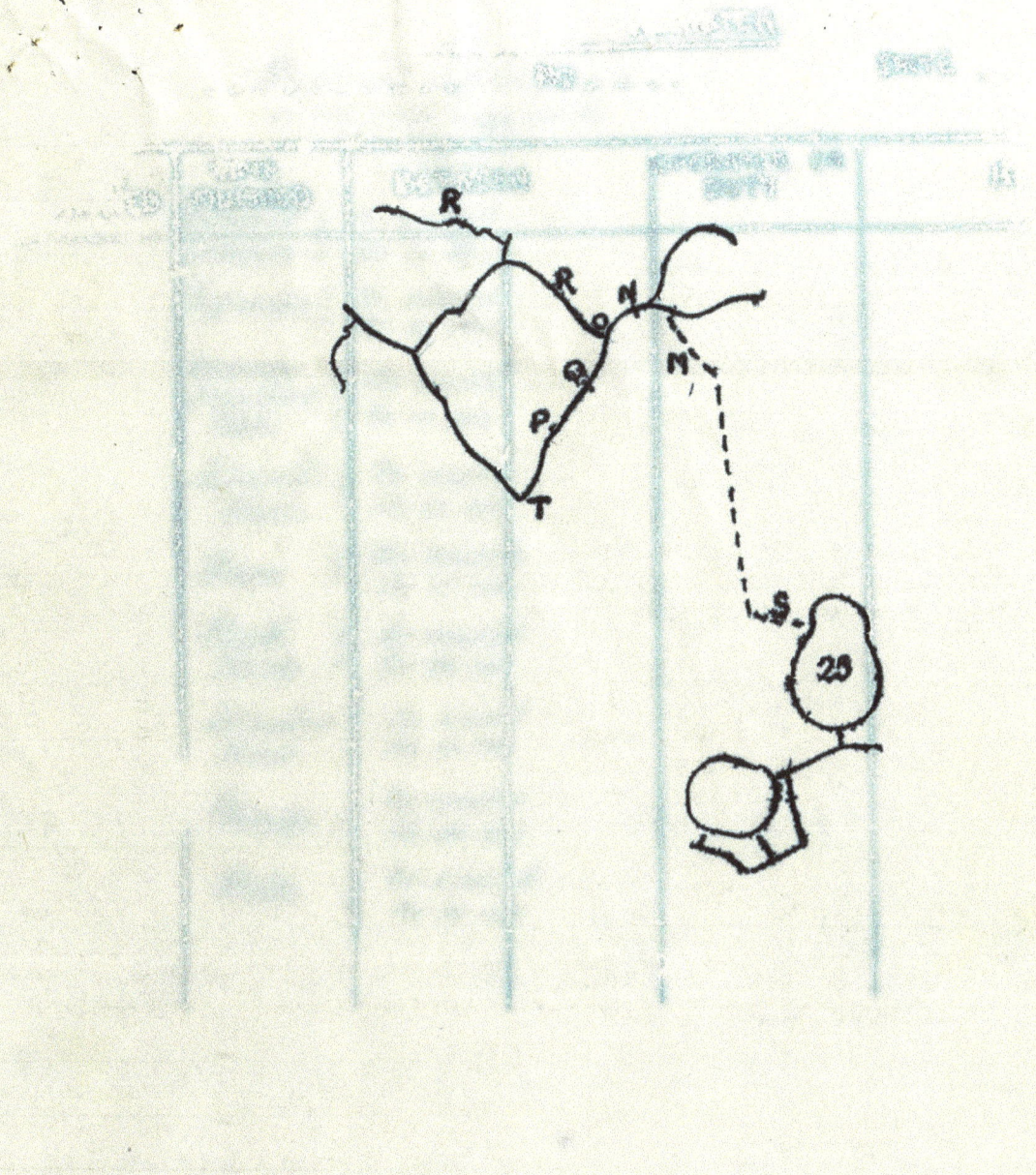

app III

attached

The C.O. in circulating the above report of the O.C. "A" Coy whilst congratulating all who took part in the rescue for their gallant behaviour, considers the following are worthy of special distinction.

        2/Lt.F.A.THEW   (Killed)

        Sergt. Cheeseman
        L/Cpl. Harvey
        Pte. Oakley
         " Watkins
         " Thomas

The following entry will be made in the Pay Book of all taking part:-

    "On the 12th September 1916, (No. Rank & Name) behaved very gallantly in the rescue of the bodies of 2 Officers under heavy fire".

                      (Signed)   C.A.LUCK

                               Lieut. Colonel.
                    Comdg. 2/22nd Bn.Lon.Regt.

21-9-16.

AMENDMENT   Copy No. 5

    Please amend Phase 1 of Appendix A of Brigade Operation
Order 17 issued to-day to read
    Guns and T.M's will open fire at ⊬ 10 minutes instead
    of ⊬ 5 minutes.

                                        [signature]
                                        Captain
                                        Brigade Major
                                        181st Infantry Bde

[Stamp: SECRET — HEADQUARTERS 181st INFANTRY BRIGADE — 5-9-16]

Appendix "A"

SCHEME FOR TRENCH MORTAR CO-OPERATION.

PHASE 1

STOKES GUN

GUN	Time of Opening fire	Time of Ceasing fire	No. of rounds to be fired	TARGET	REMARKS
Nos. 1,2, 3 & 4	/5	/8	45	Support Trench A.23.a.09.42 to A.22.b.36.92	The first 5 rounds from each gun will be air bursts. Traversing fire along the sector of trench.
Nos. 5 & 6	/5	/8	45	Support Trench A.22.b.45.50 to A.22.b.20.65	
Nos. 7 & 8	/5	/8	45	Support Trench A.16.c.85.25 to A.16.c.75.55	
Nos. 1,2, 3 & 4	/19	/21	30	Front line trench A.23.a.12.40 to A.22.b.32.95	PHASE 2 1 and 3 guns firing air bursts
Nos. 5 & 6	/19	/21	30	Support Trench A.22.b.35.50 to A.22.b.20.85	No.5 gun will fire air bursts
Nos. 7 & 8	/19	/21	30	Support Trench A.6.c.85.25 to A.16.c.75.55	No.7 gun will fire air bursts

TOTAL NUMBER OF ROUNDS 360 / 20 ROUNDS per gun EMERGENCY RESERVE = 520 ROUNDS

On completion of bombardment O.C. Batteries will be ready to assist in any emergency that may arise.

2" TRENCH MORTARS

	From	To		Phase 1	Phase 2
No. 1	/5	/20	Trench Junction	A.23.c.60.42	A.23.c.60.42
No. 2	/5	/20	"	A.22.b.90.30	A.22.b.90.30
No. 3	/5	/20	"	A.22.b.30.55	A.22.b.30.55
No. 4	/5	/20	"	A.16.c.80.40	A.16.c.80.40

Nos. 1,2,3 & 4 Cease Fire until 5 minutes All mortars on same trenches (time unknown) afterwards in Phase 1

SECRET

2/22nd Bn London Regt.

Vol 5.

WAR DIARY
for
OCTOBER
1916

From 1st October 1916
To 31st October 1916.

VOLUME . I .

WAR DIARY or INTELLIGENCE SUMMARY

Army Form C. 2118

(Erase heading not required.)

Instructions regarding War Diaries and Intelligence Summaries are contained in F.S. Regs., Part II. and the Staff Manual respectively. Title Pages will be prepared in manuscript.

Place	Date	Hour	Summary of Events and Information	Remarks and references to Appendices
ECURIE	1/10/16		2nd Lt. S. H. Blakey joined the Bn. from the 22nd Res. Bn.	J.7.H.
"	2/10/16		Nothing to report.	J.7.H.
"	3/10/16		2nd Lts. C.J. Dyke, L.N. Bonnell and G.C.F. James joined the Bn. from the 22nd Res. Bn.	J.7.H.
"	4/10/16		Bn. relieved 2/24 Lond. R. in Right II. Relief completed without casualty. See App. I. Our 2" T.M.s began cutting enemy wire between A.16.C.7 & A.16.C.7 6.30 & continued doing so until the morning of the 8th. 2nd Lt. J. A. Berney joined Bn. from 22nd Res. Bn.	App. I J.7.H.
POST LILLE	5/10/16			J.7.H.
"	6/10/16		No incident to report.	J.7.H.
"	7/10/16		3 gaps reported in enemy wire near A.16.C.7.4 & 2nd Lt. D.J. Goldring joined Bn. from 22nd Res. Bn.	J.7.H.
"	8/10/16	6.5 p.m.	A raid was undertaken on the enemy front line & communication trenches between A.16.C.7 0.4.8 & A.16.C.7 6.30. The party returned at 6.25 p.m. with 2 J.7.H. 4 prisoners, having bombed 7 dug-outs known to be occupied & killed 5 Germans. Little resistance was offered but a heavy hostile barrage was put over 30 minutes after the party started. Capt. Colmer was in charge of the operation, & 2nd Lt. Cronkholm commanded the whole raiding party; 2nd Lt. J.7.H. Lts Hayford & Brassey & 2nd Lt. Weston each commanded parties, which were drawn from the whole battalion. The total raiding party consisted of 4 officers, 8 N.C.O.s & 44 men. For casualties see appendix.	App. II J.7.H.

WAR DIARY
or
INTELLIGENCE SUMMARY

(Erase heading not required.)

Army Form C. 2118

Place	Date	Hour	Summary of Events and Information	Remarks and references to Appendices
POST LILLE	8/10/16	6.3 p.m.	A feint raid was undertaken on A.22.b. 05.70. The team of which were a smoke barrage & a bombardment with Stokes guns of crater XX. Capt. McComas & 2nd Lt. Arnold were in charge of these operations, which successfully drew the enemy's fire & caused commotion in the German lines. Casualties – Wounded 2nd Lt. Arnold & 4 O.R. One other casualty – Killed O.R. – was sustained in the course of the night. Nothing to report.	J.J.H.
"	9/10/16		Bn. was relieved in Right II by 2/24 Lond. R. & went into Divisional Reserve at Étrun.	J.J.H.
"	10/10/16		Relief completed without casualty.	APP III J.J.H.
ÉTRUN	10/10/16 to 16/10/16		Bn. in Divisional Reserve. J.J.H. 12/10/16 Lt. W.R. Phillips transferred to R.F.C.	J.J.H.
"	13/10/16		Bn. was inspected by Major-General E.S. Bulfin C.B. C.V.O. Commanding 60th (London) Division.	J.J.H.
"	15/10/16		2995 L/Cpl Harrison, 4923 Pte Hocking, & 3330 Pte Cassidy were awarded the Military Medal in connection with the raid on the 8th inst.	APP IV J.J.H.
"	16/10/16		Bn. relieved 2/24 Lond. R. in Right II; relief was completed without casualty by 9 P.M.	J.J.H.
POST LILLE	17/10/16		Artillery fired at A.16.b. & A.16.d, & at suspected T.M. emplacement at A.22.a.85.45; enemy did some damage to B.onal with T.M.'s in the afternoon.	App V J.J.H.
"	18/10/16		Continued firing on enemy T.M. emplacements.	J.J.H.

Army Form C. 2118

WAR DIARY
or
INTELLIGENCE SUMMARY
(Erase heading not required.)

Instructions regarding War Diaries and Intelligence Summaries are contained in F.S. Regs., Part II. and the Staff Manual respectively. Title Pages will be prepared in manuscript.

Place	Date	Hour	Summary of Events and Information	Remarks and references to Appendices
POST LILLE	19/10/16		A draft of 35 N.C.O.'s & men joined the Bn. from the 3rd line.	J.F.H
"	20/10/16		No incident to report.	J.F.H
"	21/10/16		Announcement made that Capt. G. J. Colmer had been awarded the Military Cross in connexion with the raid on the 8th inst.	J.F.H APP.6
"	22/10/16		Firing at hostile T.M. emplacements	J.F.H
"	23/10/16		No incident to report.	J.F.H
"	24/10/16		Bn. relieved by 1st Canadian Mounted Rifles & went back to billets at Étrun	Att. 7 J.F.H
ÉTRUN	25/10/16		Bn. marched to Izel-Les-Hameau, starting at 9.30 a.m.	J.F.H
IZEL-LES-HAMEAU	26/10/16		Bn. marched to Rebreuviette.	Att. 8 J.F.H
REBREUVI-ETTE	27/10/16		Bn. rested.	
"	28/10/16		Bn. marched to Neuvillette	J.F.H
NEUVILLETTE	29/10/16		Bn. marched to Candas.	J.F.H
CANDAS	30/10/16		Bn. rested at Candas	J.F.H
"	31/10/16		Bn. rested at Candas.	J.F.H

OC 2/2 Bn Lincoln Regt

App. I

2/2nd London Regt.   O A g M,6
Order No 22.   App I

1. The 2/2 London Regt will be relieved by the 2/3rd London Regt on the afternoon of the 4th inst and will themselves relieve the 2/24th London Regt in the front line.

2. Companies will be in the following position in the line —
   A coy in Support
   B "   in the Centre
   C "   on the Right
   D "   on the Left.

3. OC coys will send on the usual details in advance and will send in to Bn HQ ECURIE the usual list of trench stores signed by both incoming + outgoing OC coys before moving off.

4. Usual departmentals will relieve in advance.

5. The /2 Lond R will start to relieve the /2 London R about 2.30pm

6. Completion of relief will be notified to Bn HQ by the code
   TWO of EACH

7. ACKNOWLEDGE

Copies to 2/rd B.   A Mayer Capt + Adjt
         OC MGCP +2°   2/2nd Lond Regt.
         Lewis Gun Officer
         Signalling Officer
         War Diary

Headquarters,
181st Infantry Brigade.

App II

        I have to report the following points from last night's raid carried out by this Battalion.

There is no doubt that the German front line trenches and dug-outs were full of men, indications point to a large working party assembled in readiness to repair wire and trenches after dark.

5 Germans are known to have been killed whilst escaping over the top back to their support line and 7 dug-outs known to be occupied were bombed with at least ten bombs apiece. One dug-out in which there were several Germans in their shirt sleeves collapsed.

I have to report that the behaviour of all ranks was all that could be desired.

The initial advance never hesitated and kept right up to own barrage thereby being subjected to no opposition.

The subsequent operations were carried out according to programme and all the different parties carried out their allotted duties and returned as pre-arranged.

    I propose bringing the names of several who took part to your notice.

                                       MAJOR.
                            Commanding 2/22nd Battalion London Regiment.

9-10-16.

List of Casualties sustained on the
night of the Raid 8-10-16.

-:-:-:-:-:-:-:-:-:-:-:-:-:-

"B" Coy:-   2237 Pte.Jacques G.J.   Killed
            5507 " Jolly H.G.   Missing
            LIEUT.N.M.HAYFORD   Wounded
            4812 L/Cpl.Barden T.L.   Wounded - Shell Shock.
            3461   "   Ellis H.S.C.   "
            4848 Pte.Schroder S.W.   "
     5499   " Kemp F.   "
            4960 " Croad H.T.   "   With Company.

"C" Coy:-   2/Lt.E.B.WESTON   Wounded
            2/Lt.E.E.ARNOLD   "
            4798 L/Sgt.Curtis G.H.   "
     4813   L/Cpl.Montgomery H.   "
            7074 Pte.Muggleton C.   "

            5733 Pte.Reedman O.V.   Killed   ) During
            3132 " Warrier   Shell Shock) Duncan

"D" Coy:-   Capt.G.J.COLMER   Wounded
            3442 Pte.Ellery G.   Killed
            7086 " Tricker G.   Killed
            1467 Sgt.Murrell B.   Wounded
            5043 Pte.Stanbridge H.C   "
            5031 " Warburton W.E.   "
            3644 " Holton J.W.   "
            3799 L/Cpl.Lee E.A.   "
            7079 Pte.Reed D.H.   "
            5557 " Wren R.C.   "
            3340 " Gosby A.E.   "
            5022 " Hutchings A.H.   "   returned to duty
            2615 " Barrett D.   Shell Shock
            4091 L/Cpl.Anderson B.J.   Wounded

-:-:-:-:-:-:-:-:-:-:-:-:-:-:-:-:-

A report on the events leading up to and subsequent to the deaths of:-

2/LT.G.I.KINROSS   and   2/LT.F.A.THEW.

At 7-20 a.m. on September 12th LT.KINROSS left our advanced crater XIV in company with Pte.THOMAS to carry out a reconnaissance, Runner HUBBARD was in attendance.

The party proceeded thro' Crater XII which they left by its northern sap, at this point LT.KINROSS instructed Pte.THOMAS to proceed towards the LILLE ROAD while he himself struck off to the left.

Before moving off he said to his runner Pte.HUBBARD "I shall go and have another look, but I shall not want you", referring to Craters XIX and XIXA which he and Pte.HUBBARD had already reconnoitred early that morning and had been sniped at while so doing.

What precisely was in LT.KINROSS' mind can only be inferred.

It would appear that his earlier reconnaissance failed to satisfy him and that, scenting danger he preferred to investigate further unattended.

In due course Pte.THOMAS returned to our advanced crater XIV and finding LT.KINROSS had not returned, he at once went out again accompanied with L/Cpl.HARVEY.

After some difficulty they located LT.KINROSS lying on the inner lip of Crater XIX A.

L/Cpl.HARVEY then went out over the lip of the crater to his assistance and found him badly wounded and unconscious.

L/Cpl.HARVEY called for help which Pte.THOMAS promptly rendered, and between them they drew LT.KINROSS several feet nearer the lip of the crater, while thus engaged about 12 shots were fired at them from the further lip of Crater XIX, where about 6 of the enemy were discerned.

At this stage a bullet glancing off a bomb in Pte.THOMAS' hand wounded him in the side.

L/Cpl.HARVEY thus unaided was unable to move LT.KINROSS so assisted Pte.THOMAS who showed signs of collapse, back over the lip and towards our own line.

On reaching Sap 28 they met runner HUBBARD and Cpl.HARVEY informed him that LT.KINROSS was seriously wounded and Pte.THOMAS hit.

Pte.HUBBARD immediately doubled back to LT.THEW's dug-out and reported what he had heard.

Leaving instructions to communicate the news to Capt.RICHARDSON at Coy. H.Q. LT. THEW returned with all haste to our advanced crater.

This message was received by Capt.RICHARDSON at 7-40 a.m.

LT.THEW taking Sgt.CHEESEMAN, 6 men and 2 stretcher bearers then proceeded to LT.KINROSS led by L/Cpl.HARVEY.

On arrival at the near side of the crater-lip where LT.KINROSS lay a covering party of six men was thrown out with orders to bring rapid converging fire to bear on the enemy post.

LT.THEW and L/Cpl.HARVEY then tried to draw LT.KINROSS over by his feet but any movement they produced only served to draw the enemy fire to that point.

LT.THEW observing this rose, fired his revolver, sprang over the lip of the crater, seized LT.KINROSS bodily and dragged him back over the lip, at this point he was himself fatally hit, and retaining his grasp fell back bringing LT.KINROSS with him, thus accomplishing the most dangerous part of the task.

During this time the covering party maintained a steady rate of fire, the steadiness of Ptes.OAKLEY and WATKINS under a heavy fire being most noticeable.

From this point, Sgt.CHEESEMAN took over command, and I consider it was due to his coolness and foresight that LTS.KINROSS and THEW were brought in and the covering party gradually withdrawn without casualty.

Sgt.CHEESEMAN was the last one to return. This all took place in broad daylight within 20 yards of the German lines.

                (Signed)   GUY. F. RICHARDSON Capt.

                                      O.C."A" Company.

The following is a list of the names of those who acted as covering party and in other capacities.

    Sergt. CHEESEMAN   Cpl. BURRETT
    Pte. FLINT   Pte. HUBBARD (Runner)
    " OAKLEY   L/Cpl. YOUNG
    " WATKINS   Pte. HYDE
    " TITTERINGTON   " MOULD
    " THOMAS   L/Cpl. HARVEY
Stretcher Bearer ~~Curtis~~ CURTIS
    " " L/Cpl. DALTON

    (Signed)   GUY. F. RICHARDSON
    Capt.

(In pads of 50 dupls.)   "C" Form (Duplicate).   Army Form C. 2123.

MESSAGES AND SIGNALS.

No. of Message ...27...

SM 1EPM 2C   HD   Pl Annex

Charges to Pay. £ s. d.

Office Stamp. OM 8/10/—

Service Instructions.

Handed in at ...HD... Office ......m. Received ...9.__.m.

TO   B. CATT N

Sender's Number	Day of Month	In reply to Number	AAA
SSM 28	8		

Following received from BERYL aaa
begins aaa Please investigate
MAJ BORTON and DoE
Andrewsful nurse aaa Ends

FROM   HOUND

PLACE & TIME   9.22 pm

(In pads of 50 dupls.) "C" Form (Duplicate). Army Form C. 2123.
MESSAGES AND SIGNALS. No. of Message ....

SM CORPM 19 HD
                Priority

	Charges to Pay.	Office Stamp.
	£ s. d.	CM
		8/10/16

Service Instructions.
                HD

Handed in at ...... HD ...... Office 11.30 p.m. Received 11.40 p.m.

TO   B BN

Sender's Number	Day of Month	In reply to Number	A A A
SC 767	8		

CORPS Commander wires to hear of it is
delighted   success   your

FROM
PLACE & TIME   HOUND
                 11.35 pm.

SUPPLEMENTARY TO PRELIMINARY REPORT
of the 2/22nd Battalion London Regiment's
Raid.   8th October 1916.

Sergt. SNELL - RIGHT BLOCK.

When we got to our position, 8 Germans who had apparently been lying in a hole just behind the Trench, got up and tried to run back to their Support line. They were bombed and at least 4 dropped. A Bosche was found with his head in a hole and was pulled out by the feet and taken back and made a prisoner. I kept my position until the order of Recall was given.

Sergt. NICHOLLS & Cpl. PULLEN - LEFT BLOCK.

On our way to the left post we came on 3 dug-outs in darkness and there were cries of "Kamerade" from all 3, but we could not get them to come out. We chucked about 30 bombs down and took one prisoner who we had to knock on the head as he refused to come.

Pte. BROAD with Centre Party advanced up the Centre Trench. They took one prisoner at once, 2 dug-outs were bombed as they could not get the Germans to come out, one of these dug-outs was connected underground with a sniper's post from which we were fired at, so we pushed a bomb down each loophole and waited to hear it explode.

MAJOR

Commanding 2/22nd Battn. London Regiment.

9-10-16.

SECRET

PRELIMINARY REPORT of the 2/22ND BATTALION
LONDON REGIMENT'S RAID. 8-10-16

Punctually at 6-3 p.m. the feint bombardment started, the basis of which was Smoke Bombs, immediately whistles and horns were distinctly heard in the German lines. This excitement was probably caused by the smoke bombs being mistaken for gas.

At 6-5 p.m. the Artillery Barrage opened and the raiding party left the OLD FRENCH Trench, all were clear by 6-8 p.m.

They moved across right up to and in fact almost in the barrage, picking up two prisoners in a saphead en route.

The wire was found to be beautifully cut and there was no necessity to use the blankets. A gap of about 30 yards having been made with only one or two gooseberries and bits of loose wire remaining.

2/Lt.CRONHELM and 6 men moved straight along the sap and entered the German trench at junction of sap and front line where he established his report centre. He then waited for the right and left bombing blocks who came up immediately.

RIGHT PARTY.

The right bombing block turned right handed down the German front line followed immediately by 2/Lt.WESTON'S party. They reached their objectives without any difficulties about 7 or 8 dug-outs were bombed. A German was shot and another unwounded German captured. On the recall signal the whole party withdrew. 2/Lt.WESTON was apparently hit whilst in the trench, an artery near the groin being severed. On withdrawing the whole party reported to 2/Lt.CRONHELM.

LEFT PARTY.

The left blocking party was sent along the trench left handed by 2/Lt.CRONHELM but got into the open as the trench was so flattened as to be unrecognisable. Here they were joined by 2/Lt.BRASSEY'S party who had also crossed the Trench. Both parties went on till some fairly thick wire was encountered and from there bombed the support German trench. On returning a wounded German was picked up in the front trench. The party then having bombed 2 or 3 dug-outs in front line trench returned on recall signal to the OLD FRENCH trench.

CENTRE PARTY.

The Centre party under Lt.HAYFORD moved straight up past their objective to the support line which they found to be a deep well duck boarded trench. They did not go down it but retired about 10 yards and made a block. Here the Germans made a bombing attack on them, wounding Lt.HAYFORD slightly in the head and 2 other men. On the recall they retired. Whilst moving up they had bombed a dug-out, presumably occupied as a bomb was thrown out. Lt.HAYFORD knowing prisoners had been taken contented himself with bombing it and did not allow his party to go in much as they wanted to.

At 6-25 p.m. (recall) 2/Lt.CRONHELM having had Lt.HAYFORD'S and WESTON'S parties report to him on their way back, went in search of Lt.BRASSEY'S party and to see if there were any others left behind. Finding no one and seeing no activity except German bombs being thrown, he retired to the OLD FRENCH trench with his runners who were with the greatest difficulty persuaded to leave the German trenches.

Captain COLMER who was established in the OLD FRENCH trench with an advanced telephone station, was wounded and the two men killed, in fact the majority of the casualties appear to have occurred in or near this trench on the return of the party.

ACTION BY THE ENEMY.

Extremely slight opposition to the raiding party in the German trenches.

S.O.S. fired at 6-23 no action until 6-35 p.m. when a 77 mm barrage was placed on 500 CRATER all along the BONNAL, 500 AVENUE and COLLECTEUR, Aerial torpedoes on SUTHERLAND AVENUE. OILCANS on CENTRE 1 front, RIFLE grenades on OLD FRENCH trench Barrage ceased at 7-10 p.m. when the only M.G. heard on raid sector opened apparently from Crater xxxiii.

GERMAN TRENCHES

Front line trench extraordinarily knocked about not duck boarded but dry.
Communication Trench not duckboarded, very wide, from 6-8 feet deep, dry.

SUPPORT TRENCH.

From what could be seen duckboarded, deep and in good condition.

CASUALTIES

Officers: Capt. COLMER wounded in thigh by rifle grenade.
Lt. HAYFORD wounded slightly by bomb splinter in the head.
2/Lt. WESTON badly wounded in thigh.

Other Ranks: 2 men killed by shell fire, 5 men wounded, 10 men slightly wounded, 1 man missing (apparently this man who had been previously wounded in the German communication trench had to be left by the man who was helping him out who whilst doing so was himself badly wounded. This information was not obtained for some considerable time afterwards.

GENERAL.

The whole operation went through without a check, all parties moving straight to their objective without any hesitation. The men behaved extremely well and in fact had to be restrained from trying to push on to the second line. The Smoke bombs were from the Trench Mortars were most accurate and were invaluable by drawing the main volume of Artillery, Trench Mortar and Machine Gun fire well away from the scene of the main operation, for certainly the first 20 minutes.

MAJOR.
Commanding 2/22nd Battalion London Regiment.

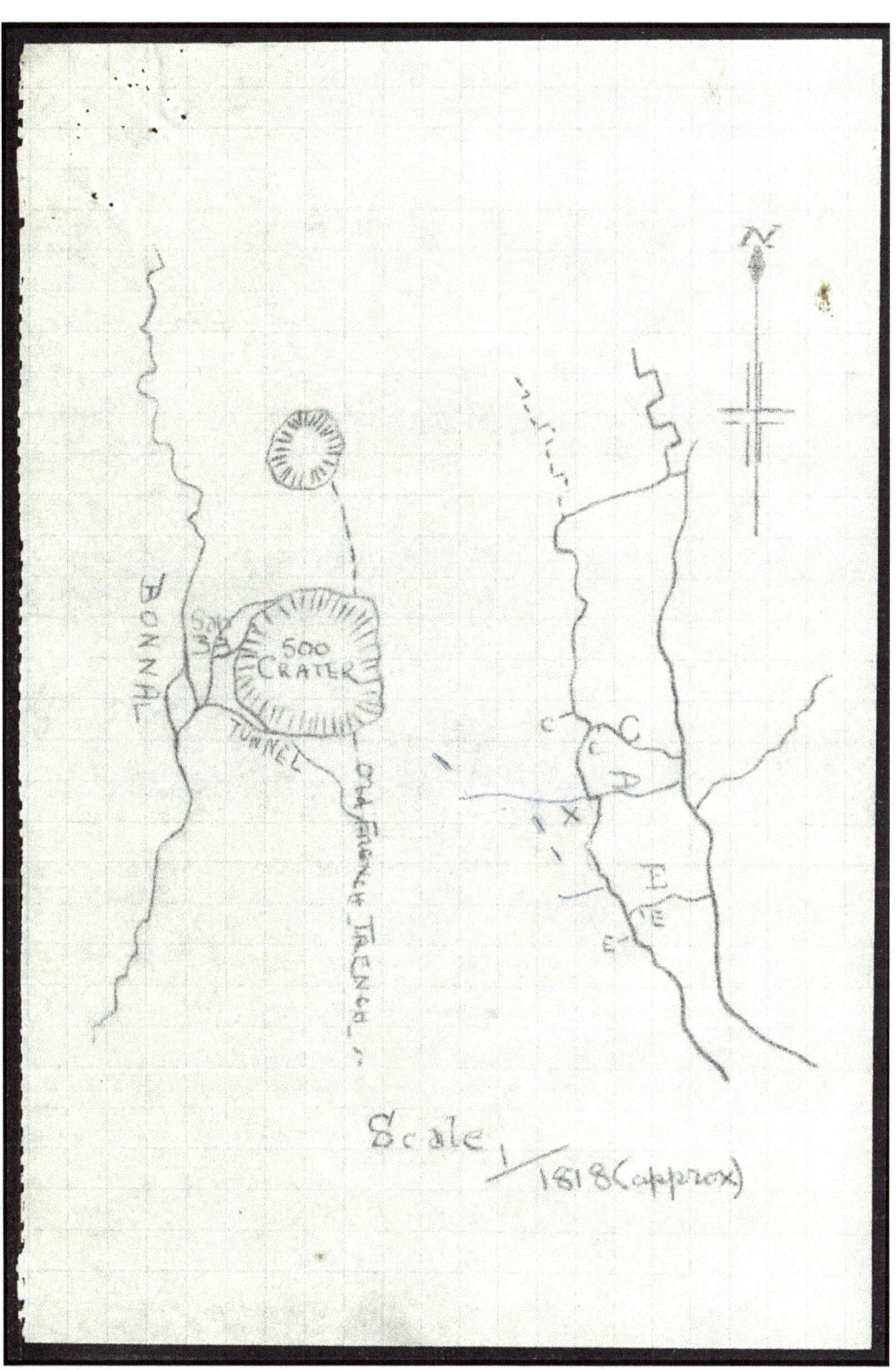

Ref: attached Map.

To be returned to Bn HQ before starting

2/22nd Battalion London Regiment.

OPERATION ORDER No. 1.
----

1. INFORMATION   The Battalion will raid the hostile front line
                  between A & B including the Sap leading therefrom.

2. OBJECTS   (i) To obtain a living prisoner.
                  (ii) To establish identification.
                  (iii) To do the greatest damage possible.

3. ZERO   Time and date to be notified later.

4. HOSTILE WIRE   Hostile wire on raid sector and on A22b.05.70
                  (approximate) is being dealt with by T.M's, see
                  Appendix B.

5. OUR OWN WIRE   The necessary gaps in our own wire are in
                  preparation. Lt.HUNTINGTON is responsible for
                  this.

6. COMMAND   Capt.COLMER will be in command and will establish
                  himself at the eastern end of tunnel at - 1 hr.

7. STRENGTH   Raiding party composed as under:-
                  Left party 2/Lt.BRASSEY 1 N.C.O. 6 men
                  Centre " Lt.HAYFORD 1 N.C.O. 8 men
                  Right   " 2/Lt.WESTON 1 N.C.O. 6 men
                  Blanket & Ladder Party 1 N.C.O. 6 men) Under
                  Left Bombing Block 1 N.C.O. 6 men   ) 2/Lt.
                  Right Bombing Block 1 N.C.O. 6 men   ) Cronhelm.
                  Rear Party 2 N.C.os 6 men.
                  Total Strength 4 Officers, 8 N.C.Os 44 men.

8. ASSEMBLY   Mine Shaft near Left Company's advanced Head-
   POINT.   quarters, Five Hundred Avenue.
                  Parties will proceed to French Trench via the
                  tunnel at - 1 hr. in the following order:-
                        Right Party
                        Centre Party
                        Left Party
                        Right Bombing Block
                        Blanket & Ladder Men
                        Left Bombing Block
                        Rear Party.

9. ADVANCE &   At Zero, the entire raiding party less Rear
   ASSAULT.   Party will advance. The Blanket Party covered
                  by Right and Left Blocking parties must reach
                  the enemy wire slightly in advance of remainder.
                  The Blanket men will bridge any part of enemy's
                  wire still remaining uncut and remainder of
                  raiding party will go through them. No local
                  hostile bombing is to be allowed to interfere
                  with the advance through the wire. The Blanket
                  men and Bombing Blocks will be under the
                  immediate command of 2/Lt.CRONHELM who will
                  subsequently establish a report centre at
                  junction of Trench D and German front line. He
                  will be responsible for the passing back to the
                  rear, of any prisoners or our own wounded and will
                  also see that passages through the wire are

(1)

9. ADVANCE & ASSAULT. (Contd)	marked and improved prior to the Recall Signal. To assist him he will have 2 men as runners in addition to the Blanket men. The Right Blocking Party will move straight to junction of Trench E and Enemy front line. They will establish Bombing Posts at cc. The Left Blocking Party will move straight to junction of Trench C and Enemy front line. They will establish similar Bombing posts at cc. Right and Left Raiding parties search and clean up front line from junction of Trench D to cc and cc respectively. Centre party will work up Trench D clean out dug-outs found, killing or capturing occupants. O.C. this party will use his discretion in selecting a place for a Bombing Block to cover his operations.
10. RECALL	At + 90 minutes Officers and N.C.Os in charge of parties will withdraw their parties, reporting to 2/Lt. CRONHELM at Report Centre en route. They will then make their way to the Point of Assembly by the shortest possible routes using their own discretion as to the safety of their men. Should there be a heavy barrage at BONNAL TRENCH, temporary shelter may be taken in the French Trench. On arrival at Assembly position a roll will be called and any description of booty will be handed over to Lt. HUNTINGTON.
11. COMMUNICAT -ION.	A telephone will be installed in the old French Trench and will be in communication with Battalion and Company Headquarters. Additional communication by runners throughout.
12. DRESS.	Skeleton equipment and pouches. Rifles charged, 9 rounds in magazine, 20 in pouches, one bomb in each pocket. 2 men in each bombing group will carry canvas buckets full of bombs. These men will carry a life preserver instead of a rifle. Shorts are not to be worn. For the purpose of recognition all ranks will wear a piece of white tape round the left shoulder strap. No regimental badges or buttons to be worn, and no papers carried which could possibly lead to identification by the enemy. Identity discs will not be worn. Companies will be responsible that the men;s pay books are collected before going to the Point of Assembly.
13. ADVANCED DRESSING STATION.	An advanced Dressing Station will be established by Capt. ASTBURY who will be responsible for all arrangements of evacuating casualties from that station.
14. DISCIPLINE	All ranks to be thoroughly warned that indiscriminate and undirected bombing will hinder and not assist the advance. Also that casualties cannot be attended to during the advance, but every effort will be made to collect and bring in casualties after the Recall. All ranks are further warned that our own barrage fire may appear very close but there will be no danger from it. In the event of their being taken prisoner, no information beyond their rank and name need be given.

(3)

15. FEINT ATTACK	A feint attack will take place on the Right Company's front at approximately A22b.05.75 see Appendices C & D. Capt.A.McCOMAS will be in general command of these operations.
16. SIGNAL OF RECALL	At + 20 Machine Guns will fire their usual rat a tat and "Very" lights will be sent up from the Sausage Redoubt at ECURIE.
17 Note.	*acknowledge* (All N.C.Os in charge of parties will be supplied with luminous watches, and will be synchronized at the Assembly position.

Copies to all concerned.

                                        MAJOR.

             Commanding 2/22nd Battalion London Regiment.

7-10-16.

5/28nd Battalion London Regiment.

APPENDIX "A"

ARTILLERY.

TIME TABLE — Zero an intense bombardment of enemy's front line A B for 25 seconds.
+30 minutes bombardment until "Cease Fire" on co-ordinates selected by O.C. Right Group.

APPENDIX "B".

2 inch TRENCH MORTAR

Previous to the raid both Trench Mortar guns employed in cutting wire in front of A B.

APPENDIX "C".

3 inch TRENCH MORTARS.   6 guns.

A & B Guns approx. A22b.05.15. — Commence firing at −3 and will fire gunfire for 3 minutes. Target Crater xx and front line behind this crater. 120 rounds.

C Gun A22a.50.65. — At Zero will fire gunfire for 30 secs. on Crater xxxiii. 10 rounds. At +30 will fire gunfire for 3 minutes traversing on enemy's front line between A16c.90.15 to A16c.93.07. 60 rounds.

D & E Guns in BONNAL between GREEN AVENUE & ORR AVENUE. — At Zero both will fire for 3 minutes gunfire (traversing searching fire) between A16c.85.20 and A16c.93.07. 120 rounds.

F Gun in BONNAL just to left of E Gun. — From +3 will fire at a slow rate of fire till the Recall Signal is given. Target same as for D & E. guns. 120 rounds.

APPENDIX "D".

SMOKE TRENCH MORTARS.

Same target and rate of fire as A & B 3 inch Mortars.

War Diary. Secret

2/22ND BATTALION LONDON REGIMENT. A H. III

ORDER No.23.d/9-10-16.

1. The 2/22nd Battalion London Regiment will be relieved by the 2/24th Battalion London Regiment on the afternoon of the 10th inst. and will proceed to Divisional Reserve.

2. The leading platoon of the 2/24th Battalion London Regiment will pass ANZIN CHURCH by 3 o'clock.

3. The same Billets at ETRUN will be occupied by Companies as before.

4. Arrangements for Baths will be issued later.

5. O.C. Companies will arrange to send down as much Stores as possible with rations tonight.

6. Completion of relief will be reported by the code DIXIES RECEIVED.

7. Acknowledge.

(Signed) ALFRED MAYER
Captain & Adjutant,
2/22nd Battn. London Regiment.

60th (LONDON) DIVISION ROUTINE ORDERS.

15th October, 1916.

PART I.

Nil.

E.T. HUMPHREYS,
Lieut. Colonel,
General Staff.

PART II.

1099. HONOURS AND REWARDS.

Under authority granted by His Majesty The King, the Army Corps Commander has awarded the following decorations for gallant conduct on the 8th October, 1916:-

2/22nd (County of London) Battalion, The London Regiment, (The Queen's.) (T.F.)

No. 2995 Lce.Cpl. FREDERICK BROUGHAM HARRISON - Military Medal.

Date of Award, 15th October, 1916.

Lce.Cpl. formed one of a party which raided the enemy's Trenches on the evening of the 8th October, 1916. He was one of the first to enter the Trenches, and by his dash was instrumental in taking two German prisoners. After his Officer had been wounded, he took command of his party and showed great coolness and resource in bringing them back.

No. 4923 Pte. FRANK JAMES HOCKING - Military Medal.

Date of Award, 15th October, 1916.

Pte. Hocking formed one of a party which raided the enemy's Trenches on the evening of the 8th October, 1916. During the raid, fire was opened on the party by a German from a sniper's post with an underground entrance, which could not be discovered. He immediately dashed for the two loopholes and pushed a bomb through each, evidently killing the occupants as no further shots were fired. By this action he undoubtedly saved several casualties amongst his party.

No. 3330 Pte. HARVEY CASSIDY - Military Medal.

Date of Award, 15th October, 1916.

Pte. Cassidy formed one of a party which raided the enemy's Trenches on the evening of the 8th October, 1916. He was most conspicuous for the dash and bravery he displayed in engaging and dispersing groups of hostile bombers who were in several instances in superior numbers. He also assisted in helping in our wounded under heavy fire.

1100. CHAPLAINS - STRENGTH.

The Rev. W.F. CROSTHWAIT, C.F., (C.E.), attached 179th Infantry Brigade, having been posted to the Base, is struck off the strength of the Division accordingly.
(Authority - Asst. Chaplain General (C. of E.) A.C.C. 9/135 dated 12/10/16)

V. MALCOLM,
Lieut. Colonel,
A.A. & Q.M.G.

SECRET.

App 5

2/22nd Battalion London Regiment.

Order No. 24 d/15-10-16.

1. The 2/22nd Battalion London Regiment will relieve the 2/24th Battalion London Regiment in the Front Line on the afternoon of the 16th inst.

2. The Companies of the 2/22nd Battalion London Regiment will be disposed as follows in the Front Line of Right 11.

   "A" Coy. on the Right, "B" Coy. in the Centre,
   "D" Coy. on the Left, "C" Coy. in Support.

3. Starting Point: Bridge by BTRUN Baths.

4. The Battalion will move up to ANZIN Communication Trench by platoons at 5 minutes interval in the following order:-

   "A" Coy. starting at 12-30 p.m.   "B" Coy. starting at 12-50 p.
   "C"   "   "   1-10 "   "D"   "   "   1-30 "

5. The usual details will be sent on in advance. The relief of Lewis Guns to be completed by 10-30 a.m.

6. O.C. Companies will make their own arrangements for all ranks to have dinner before moving off.

7. Completion of relief will be acknowledged by the Code "BISCUITS INFECTED".

8. Acknowledge.

            (Signed)   ALFRED MAYER

                            Captain & Adjutant.
                            2/22nd Battalion London Regiment.

Copies issued to:-

   No. 1. War Diary
       2. O.C., 2/24th Bn.Lon.Regt.
       3. O.C., "A" Coy
       4. O.C., "B" "
       5. O.C., "C" "
       6. O.C., "D" "
       7. O.C., Signal Section.
       8. O.C., Lewis Gun Section.
       9. Quartermaster.

   Please note that the time of the relief may be altered to later in the afternoon; in the event of any alteration this will be notified to you in the morning.

15th October 1916.

SECRET.

In connection with the Relief Orders, the time of passing the Bridge at ETRUN Baths is altered to:-

"A" Coy 4-30 p.m.
"B" "   4-50   "
"D" "   5-10   "
"C" "   5-30   "

FROM THE ADJUTANT.

16-10-16.

60th (LONDON) DIVISION ROUTINE ORDERS.

21st October, 1916.

PART I.

Nil.

E.T. HUMPHREYS,
Lieut. Colonel,
General Staff.

PART II.

1115. HONOURS AND REWARDS.

Under authority granted by His Majesty The King, the General Officer Commanding-in-Chief has awarded the following decoration for gallant conduct on the 8th October, 1916:-

2/22nd (County of London) Battalion, The London Regiment, (The Queen's) (T.F.)

Captain GRAHAM JOHN COLMER - MILITARY CROSS.

Date of Award, 19th October, 1916.

Captain Colmer was in command of the operations when the German Trenches were raided on the evening of the 8th October, 1916. By his coolness and resource, the whole operation was successfully launched and carried out. Towards the close of the raid he was badly wounded in three places, but continued at his post and directed operations. He remained out until all the party had returned, and it was greatly owing to his coolness and example that the raid was brought to a successful conclusion.

Under authority granted by His Majesty The King, the Army Corps Commander has awarded the following decorations for gallant conduct on the 9th October, 1916:-

2/17th (County of London) Battalion, The London Regiment, (Poplar and Stepney Rifles) (T.F.)

2031 Sergt. ALFRED THOMAS OLIVER - Military Medal.

Date of Award, 21st October, 1916.

Sergt. Oliver commanded a bombing party during a raid on the German Trenches on the 9th October, 1916. On entering the German Trench he attacked, single-handed, three Germans, one of whom he killed and one of whom he captured. He subsequently with a party under an officer entered a German mine shaft, but, arriving at the first gallery under the enemy's fire, found the Germans in considerable numbers. He assisted his officer to throw all the bombs the party had with them, and as the Officer commanding the raid had given the signal to return, he returned with his bombing party, covering the retirement of the rest of the men. He was one of the last men to leave the enemy's Trenches. He showed during the whole operation the greatest coolness and bravery.

HONOURS AND REWARDS (CONTD.)

3416 Sergt. JOHN BERTRAM YOUNG, 6th Inniskilling
Dragoons, attached 2/17th Battalion,

Military Medal.

Date of Award, 21st October, 1916.

During a Raid on the enemy's Trenches on the 9th October, 1916, Sergt. Young was one of the first men to enter the Trench at the head of his party. He discovered two Germans in a shelter, one of whom he shot; the other he seized and dragged over the parapet to our Lines. He again returned and searched the German Trenches. He found no further Germans but collected several articles of booty. He displayed the greatest daring and courage throughout the operation.

1116. SATCHELS - GAS HELMET.

With reference to Divisional Routine Order No. 1104 dated 18/10/16, it should be noted that on receipt of Small Box Respirators the old pattern Satchel will be returned.

In cases where the new pattern Satchel, which is larger and has two compartments, is not in possession, indents will be submitted to the D.A.D.O.S.

P. MALCOLM,
Lieut. Colonel,
A.A. & Q.M.G.

NOTICE.

LOST.

On the 23rd September, 1916, Colt Revolver, No. 39510.

Communications will be sent to Rear Headquarters, 180th Infantry Brigade.

Copy No. 7.

2/22nd Battalion London Regiment.

Order No. 25.

---

(1) The 2/22nd Battalion London Regiment will be relieved on the morning of the 24th by the 1st Canadian Mounted Rifles.

(2) O.C. Coys will detail ~~1 officer per Coy and~~ 1 guide per platoon to be at ANZIN Church at 9-30 a.m. on the 24th. *to Report to Lt Randall*

(3) Guides will bring up relieving Companies by the following routes:-
   (a) Right Coy: ANZIN AVENUE - ROCLINCOURT AVE. - FANTOME AVE.
   (b) Other 3 Coys: ANZIN AVE. - ROCADE AVE. - HIGH STREET - LABYRINTHE AVE.

(4) Routes down for 2/22nd Battalion London Regiment:
   (a) Right Coy: FANTOME - GENIE - ANZIN AVE.
   (b) Other 3 Coys: LABYRINTHE - HIGH STREET - ROCADE - ANZIN AVE.

(5) All ranks will keep to the trenches and no movement across the open east of ANZIN Church is to be permitted.

(6) O.C. Coys. will report arrival of their Companies at ETRUN to the Adjutant by runner.

(7) Baths are being arranged for Tuesday afternoon, details will be issued later.

(8) The Q.M. will arrange with Coy. Q.M.Sgts. for all ranks to have a hot meal on arrival at ETRUN on Tuesday afternoon.

(9) Completion of relief will be reported to Battalion Headquarters by the code CAMP KETTLES TEN.

(10) Acknowledge.

2/22nd Bn. London Regiment.

23-10-16.

(Signed) ALFRED MAYER

Captain & Adjutant.
2/22nd Battn. London Regiment.

Issued at 7-30 p.m.

Copy No. 1 File
        2 War Diary
        3 181st Inf. Bde.
        4 O.C., "A" Coy.
        5 O.C., "B" "
        6 O.C., "C" "
        7 O.C., "D" "
        8 O.C., 1st Canadian Mounted Rifles.

Copy No. 1 App 8

S E C R E T.

2/22nd Battalion London Regiment.

Order No. 27.

Reference Maps

    LENS 11   1/100,000
    FRANCE 51c 1/40,000

1. The 2/22nd Battalion London Regt., the 181st Machine Gun Coy. and 181st Trench Mortar Battery will move from IZEL LES HAMEAU to REBREUVIETTE on the 26th October 1916.

2. Route: MANIN - LIENCOURT - ETREE - WAMIN.

3. Starting point cross roads south of IZEL LES HAMEAU (100 yds. east of the U in HAMEAU) (reference Map LENS 11).

4. The 2/22nd Battalion London Regt. will pass the starting point at 9-15 a.m.
The 181st Machine Gun Coy. at 9-40 a.m.
The 181st Trench Mortzr Battery at 9-50 a.m.
All troops to be clear of IZEL LES HAMEAU by 10 a.m.

5. Billeting parties of the 181st Machine Gun Coy. and 181st Trench Mortar Battery will report to Lieut.J.F.HUNTINGTON 2/22nd Battalion London Regt. at the Church REBREUVIETTE at 10 a.m. on the 26th inst.

6. ACKNOWLEDGE.

                (Signed)   ALFRED MAYER

                      Captain   & Adjutant.
               2/22nd Battalion London Regiment.

Copies to: No. 1 War Diary.
            2 181st Inf. Bde.
            3 181st M.G. Coy.
            4 181st T.M.Battery
            5 O.C., "A" Coy.
            6 O.C., "B" "
            7 O.C., "C" "
            8 O.C., "D" "
            9 Quartermaster
          10 Transport Officer
          11 Filed
          12 1/12 Loyal North Lancs. Regt

WAR DIARY

CHAMBER OF ARTILLERY
2/22nd LONDON REGIMENT

Vol 6

SECRET

WAR DIARY

for the
month of
NOVEMBER
1916

FROM 1st November 1916.
TO 30th November 1916

VOLUME I.

Army Form C. 2118

WAR DIARY
or
INTELLIGENCE SUMMARY
(Erase heading not required.)

Instructions regarding War Diaries and Intelligence Summaries are contained in F.S. Regs., Part II. and the Staff Manual respectively. Title Pages will be prepared in manuscript.

Place	Date	Hour	Summary of Events and Information	Remarks and references to Appendices
CANDAS	Nov 1 to Nov 4		Bn. in rest at Candas.	J.7.H
"	Nov 4		Bn. inspected by Sir D. Haig commanding the British Armies in France.	J.7.H
"	Nov 4		Bn. marched to billets in Brucamps.	Pamp. I
BRUCAMPS	Nov 4 to Nov 24		Bn. at Brucamps.	J.7.H
"	Nov 10		2nd Lt. D.E.C. Jones joined the Bn. from the 22nd Res Bn.	J.7.H
"	Nov 24		Bn. entrained at Longpré Station to proceed to Marseilles	J.7.H
In the Train	Nov 25		Bn. in the Train.	J.7.H
"	Nov 26		Bn. arrived at Marseilles about 10 p.m. & marched to Musso Camp.	J.7.H
MUSSO	Nov 27 to Nov 30		Bn. at Musso Camp.	J.7.H

Colonel

www.ingramcontent.com/pod-product-compliance
Lightning Source LLC
Chambersburg PA
CBHW081450160426
43193CB00013B/2430